CELEBRATING THE NAME ELIZABETH

Celebrating the Name Elizabeth

Walter the Educator

Silent King Books a WhichHead Imprint

Copyright © 2024 by Walter the Educator

All rights reserved. No part of this book may be reproduced in any manner whatsoever without written permission except in the case of brief quotations embodied in critical articles and reviews.

First Printing, 2024

Disclaimer
This book is a literary work; poems are not about specific persons, locations, situations, and/or circumstances unless mentioned in a historical context. This book is for entertainment and informational purposes only. The author and publisher offer this information without warranties expressed or implied. No matter the grounds, neither the author nor the publisher will be accountable for any losses, injuries, or other damages caused by the reader's use of this book. The use of this book acknowledges an understanding and acceptance of this disclaimer.

dedicated to everyone with the first name of Elizabeth

CONTENTS

Dedication v

One - Praises Of Elizabeth 1

Two - So Divine 3

Three - Eloquence And Grace 5

Four - Garden Of Love 7

Five - Unwavering Care 9

Six - Joy And Bliss 11

Seven - Everlasting Myth 13

Eight - Elizabeth Fair 15

Nine - Every Heart 17

Ten - Forevermore 19

Eleven - Banner Of Honor 21

Twelve - Regal Aura 23

Thirteen - Etched Deeply 25

Fourteen - Stars That Shine 27

Fifteen - Elizabeth Stands Tall 29

Sixteen - Precious Than Gold 31

Seventeen - Oh, Elizabeth 33

Eighteen - Boundless Serenity 35

Nineteen - Celebrate You 37

Twenty - Reigns Supreme 39

Twenty-One - Here's To The Elizabeths 41

Twenty-Two - Roses In Bloom 43

Twenty-Three - One Of A Kind 45

Twenty-Four - Resonates 47

Twenty-Five - Glows 49

Twenty-Six - Melodic Chime 51

Twenty-Seven - Epochs And Epochs 53

Twenty-Eight - Transcending Years 55

Twenty-Nine - Odyssey In Eternity 57

Thirty - Her Name 59

Thirty-One - Sovereign 61

Thirty-Two - Legacy 63

Thirty-Three - Cheers 65

Thirty-Four - Tale To Be Told 67

Thirty-Five - Love And Power 69

About The Creator 71

ONE

PRAISES OF ELIZABETH

Elizabeth, a name so grand,
In every way, it takes a stand.
With elegance and grace, it shines,
A name that's truly one of a kind.

In gardens fair, where flowers bloom,
Elizabeth's name dispels all gloom.
Like a melody, sweet and clear,
It whispers softly to all who hear.

In the meadows where dreams take flight,
Elizabeth's name brings pure delight.
A symphony of letters, it weaves,
A tapestry of hope that never leaves.

In every tale and legend old,
Elizabeth's name is worth more than gold.

A beacon in the darkest night,
Guiding all with its radiant light.
 In every language, it rings true,
Elizabeth, a name so rare and new.
A treasure trove of sounds and hues,
A masterpiece that cannot be confused.
 So let us raise our voices high,
And sing the praises of Elizabeth nigh.
For in this name, we find our worth,
A name that's cherished above the earth.

TWO

SO DIVINE

Elizabeth, a name so divine,
In its syllables, stars align.
Like a sonnet, sweet and true,
It captures hearts, old and new.

In the gardens of time, it blooms,
A name that dispels all glooms.
With each letter, a story untold,
A name that never grows old.

In the meadows of dreams, it dances,
A name that kindles hopeful chances.
A melody that soothes the soul,
In Elizabeth's name, we find our goal.

In the annals of history, it stands,
A name that echoes across lands.
A lighthouse in the tempest's roar,
Guiding ships to a tranquil shore.

In every tongue, it holds its sway,
Elizabeth, a name that will never fray.
A mosaic of sounds and hues,
A name that inspires and imbues.

So let us raise our voices high,
And laud the name of Elizabeth nigh.
For in its letters, we find our mirth,
A name that's cherished above the earth.

THREE

ELOQUENCE AND GRACE

In the land of eloquence and grace,
There dwells a name, Elizabeth, a captivating embrace.
A symphony of syllables, a melody so divine,
In every letter, a story, a history to enshrine.

Elegance and strength intertwined,
In the name Elizabeth, a legacy defined.
From ancient realms to modern days,
Its beauty and power forever ablaze.

In the garden of names, a rare and precious bloom,
Elizabeth, a name that dispels all gloom.
Like a diamond in the rough, it shines so bright,
A beacon of hope, a guiding light.

In the tapestry of life, a name so profound,
Elizabeth, a treasure, in every sight and every sound.

A muse for poets, a muse for dreams,
In every verse, its splendor gleams.
    From the pages of history to the present stage,
Elizabeth, a name that transcends every age.
A symposium of strength, a symphony of grace,
In the name Elizabeth, a timeless embrace.
    In every heartbeat, in every breath,
Elizabeth, a name that conquers death.
A symphony of syllables, a melody so divine,
In every letter, a story, a history to enshrine.

FOUR

GARDEN OF LOVE

Elizabeth, a name so regal and grand,
Like a melody, it dances on the tongue,
In every syllable, a story is spun,
A name that echoes through time's golden sand.

In Elizabeth, a universe resides,
Each letter a star in the midnight sky,
A constellation of grace, it can't deny,
A name that in beauty, forever abides.

From Elizabeth, springs a river of hope,
A font of wisdom, a garden of love,
In every heartbeat, a message thereof,
A name that helps the weary to cope.

Oh, Elizabeth, a symphony of sound,
A tapestry of dreams, a portrait so rare,
In every whisper, a promise to care,
A name that in echoes, will always be found.

So here's to Elizabeth, a name so divine,
In every verse, it continues to shine,
A name that in every heart, will enshrine,
A timeless treasure, beyond the confines of time.

FIVE

UNWAVERING CARE

Elizabeth, a name of immense grandeur and magnificence,
Resonating like a captivating melody upon the lips,
Each syllable weaving a captivating narrative,
An appellation that resounds through the annals of time.

Within Elizabeth, an entire cosmos takes shape,
Every letter akin to a glittering celestial body,
Forming a tapestry of elegance that is undeniable,
A name that eternally embodies beauty.

From Elizabeth flows a boundless river of optimism,
A wellspring of sagacity, a lush garden of affection,
Within every heartbeat, a profound message resonates,
A name that offers solace to the disheartened.

Oh, Elizabeth, a symphony of mellifluous tones,

A masterpiece of reverie, an exceedingly rare portrait,
In every murmur, a pledge of unwavering care,
A name that reverberates endlessly.

Here's to Elizabeth, a name of unparalleled divinity,
A luminary that persists in its luminosity,
A name that eternally engraves itself in every heart,
A timeless gem that transcends the constraints of time.

SIX

JOY AND BLISS

    In realms of old, a name so bold
Elizabeth, of stories untold
A queenly grace, a gentle embrace
In every heart, her name finds its place
    Ethereal charm, like a moonlit night
Elizabeth shines, a radiant light
In whispered winds and morning dew
Her name resounds, forever true
    Elegant and wise, a timeless beauty
In every land, her name blooms with duty
A melody sung by the angels above
Elizabeth, the embodiment of love
    In gardens of dreams, her name takes flight
A symphony of hope, a guiding light
Through trials and triumphs, she stands tall
Elizabeth, the name that conquers all

With each letter, a tale to behold
In Elizabeth's name, legends unfold
A tapestry woven with threads of grace
In every corner, her name finds its place

So let us raise our voices high
In praise of Elizabeth, reaching the sky
For in her name, a legacy so grand
Elizabeth, the name that will forever stand

May this poem honor the name Elizabeth
And fill the hearts with joy and bliss

SEVEN

EVERLASTING MYTH

Elizabeth, a name so fair and bright,
In its syllables, a world of might.
A regal echo through the halls of time,
In every verse, its essence sublime.

A melody that graces the lips with ease,
A name that dances on the autumn breeze.
In whispered secrets and laughter's peal,
Elizabeth, a name that seals the deal.

With each letter, a story unfolds,
In Elizabeth's name, a saga of old.
A tapestry woven with threads of grace,
In every corner, its presence we embrace.

From ancient castles to modern days,
Elizabeth's name continues to amaze.
A beacon of strength, a symbol of grace,
In every heart, its power finds a place.

In gardens of dreams, its blooms unfurl,
A name that conquers, a precious pearl.
A legacy etched in history's scroll,
Elizabeth, a name that makes us whole.

So let us raise our voices high,
In honor of Elizabeth, reaching the sky.
For in its embrace, we find our might,
Elizabeth, a name that shines so bright.

May this ode pay homage to the name Elizabeth,
In its glory, a timeless, everlasting myth.

EIGHT

ELIZABETH FAIR

Elizabeth, a name so grand,
Resplendent like the ocean and the sand,
In letters formed, a melody is found,
A symphony of elegance, profound.

In realms of grace and pure delight,
Elizabeth shines, a star so bright,
A name that echoes through the ages,
In history's pages, it leaps and rages.

In gardens fair, where roses bloom,
Elizabeth's name dispels all gloom,
A beacon of hope, a guiding light,
A name that fills the heart with delight.

In whispers soft and laughter loud,
Elizabeth's name stands out, so proud,
It dances on the wind, a joyful sound,
In every corner, it can be found.

A name that carries strength and power,
In every triumph, in every hour,
Elizabeth, a name that stands tall,
In every heart, it will enthrall.

So here's to you, Elizabeth fair,
A name beyond compare,
In every verse and every line,
Your name will forever shine.

In every dream and every scheme,
Elizabeth, your name will gleam,
A name so rich, a name so rare,
In every heart, it will declare.

NINE

EVERY HEART

Elizabeth, a name of regal magnificence,
Like a majestic symphony of elegance,
It resonates through the annals of time,
A beacon of grace in every rhyme.

In the tapestry of history, it weaves,
A name that endures and achieves,
With each letter, a tale unfolds,
Of strength and beauty it beholds.

In fields of enchantment, it blooms,
Dispelling shadows with its graceful plumes,
A name that exudes resilience and might,
Guiding hearts through the darkest night.

In whispers and laughter, it prevails,
A name that in every moment hails,
It dances with joy in the breeze,
An anthem of triumph, a melody that frees.

Elizabeth, a name imbued with might,
A force that conquers every plight,
In every triumph, it stands tall,
Enthralling hearts, captivating all.

So here's to you, Elizabeth, so fair,
A name beyond compare,
In every verse and every line,
Your name will forever enshrine.

In every vision and every scheme,
Elizabeth, your name will gleam,
A name so opulent, a name so rare,
In every heart, it will declare.

TEN

FOREVERMORE

In the world of names, there is one that shines,
Elizabeth, a name that's truly divine,
It carries a meaning that's rare and true,
A name so full of grace, like the morning dew.

In ancient tales, it was a name of queens,
A symbol of strength, in regal scenes,
Elizabeth, a name that echoes power,
A name that stands tall like a timeless tower.

It speaks of promise, of abundance and oath,
A name that embodies loyalty and growth,
In the tapestry of life, it weaves a story,
Of resilience, courage, and boundless glory.

Elizabeth, a name that's rich and profound,
A melody of elegance, so resound,
It captures the essence of beauty and might,
A name that fills the heart with pure delight.

So let's raise a toast to this name so grand,
Elizabeth, a name that will always stand,
In the symphony of names, it holds a special place,
A name that's a masterpiece, full of grace.

In every letter, in every sound,
Elizabeth, a name that knows no bound,
For in this name, there's a world to explore,
A name that's worth cherishing, forevermore.

ELEVEN

BANNER OF HONOR

Of noble birth, she stands, Elizabeth,
In regal grace, her presence a marvel,
A name that echoes through the corridors of time,
Resounding with strength, wisdom, and beauty,
Her essence, a tapestry of virtues woven together.

Elizabeth, a name that carries the weight of history,
A lineage of queens, warriors, and pioneers,
Each bearing the name like a banner of honor,
A name that speaks of resilience and fortitude,
A symphony of syllables that sing of triumph.

In the gardens of language, her name blooms,
A rare and precious flower, rich in symbolism,
Each letter a brushstroke in a masterpiece,
Creating a portrait of elegance and sophistication,
A name that whispers of grace and grandeur.

Elizabeth, a name that dances on the lips,

A melody that enchants and captivates,
A name that evokes visions of strength and grace,
An embodiment of power and poise,
A name that resonates with timeless splendor.
    In the tapestry of existence, she is Elizabeth,
A name that weaves through the fabric of life,
A name that inspires and elevates,
A name that embodies the very essence of nobility,
A name that shines with a brilliance all its own.

TWELVE

REGAL AURA

Oh, Elizabeth, your name so fair,
In elegance and grace beyond compare.
With every syllable, a melody rings,
A symphony of beauty that forever sings.

From ancient times to modern days,
Elizabeth, your name in history stays.
A regal aura, a timeless charm,
A name that weathers every storm.

In gardens blooming with roses sweet,
The name Elizabeth is a true royal treat.
Like a diamond sparkling in the light,
Your name shines with all its might.

From Shakespeare's quill to the poet's pen,
Elizabeth, your name is praised again.
A tapestry woven with threads of gold,
A name that stands out bold and bold.

So here's to you, Elizabeth, so dear,
A name that brings joy and cheer.
In every letter, in every sound,
Your name is a treasure that's truly profound.
So raise a toast to Elizabeth's name,
A beacon of beauty, a flame of fame.
In every language, in every land,
Elizabeth, your name will always stand.

THIRTEEN

ETCHED DEEPLY

Elizabeth, a moniker so magnificent,
Like the boundless sea, immense and resplendent,
A name that reverberates across the centuries,
In the colorful annals of history's memories.

In floral gardens, she blooms as a captivating rose,
In the realm of knowledge, she's the one who knowingly knows,
Her laughter, akin to a glistening, babbling brook,
In every silhouette, she's a radiant, shimmering look.

In every narrative, her name echoes with resonance,
In every spirit, her elegance forms a protective fence,
A name that gleams like the dew at dawn's first light,
In every expanse of sky, a hue of cerulean so bright.

Elizabeth, a symphony of syllables that gracefully unfold,
In every nook and cranny, her presence is manifold,

A name that glimmers like the sun's luminous rays,
In every passing moment, a steadfast guiding blaze.
    So let's raise a glass to Elizabeth's illustrious name,
A moniker steeped in warmth, and folklore's enchanting flame,
In every soul, she's an integral, cherished part,
A name that's etched deeply within every beating heart.

FOURTEEN

STARS THAT SHINE

Oh, Elizabeth, with eyes so bright,
Your name brings joy and pure delight.
In every letter, in every sound,
A symphony of beauty is found.

Elegant and graceful, like a swan in flight,
Your name shines like a beacon in the night.
In the garden of names, you stand tall,
A precious gem among them all.

The "E" begins with energy and zeal,
A spark that ignites an eternal appeal.
"L" whispers of love and light,
A guiding star in the darkest night.

"I" is for intelligence and insight,
A mind that soars to incredible heights.
"Z" zips through the sky with zeal,
A zest for life that's truly real.

"A" dances with grace and allure,
A name that's timeless and pure.
"B" brings brilliance and boundless grace,
A name that no one can replace.
"E" echoes with echoes of empathy and ease,
A soul as gentle as the summer breeze.
"T" trembles with truth and trust,
A name that's cherished, fair, and just.
"H" hums with hope and harmony,
A name that's filled with sweet serenity.
Elizabeth, your name is a work of art,
A masterpiece that captures every heart.
In every syllable and every line,
Your name shines brighter than the stars that shine.

FIFTEEN

ELIZABETH STANDS TALL

Elizabeth, a name so regal and refined,
A moniker that echoes through the corridors of time,
A symphony of syllables, a melody of grace,
In every letter, an elegance you can trace.

From the gardens of England to the streets of Rome,
Elizabeth, a name that feels like coming home,
With a strength that echoes through the ages,
A name that's written on history's pages.

In the twilight, Elizabeth's name glows,
Like a rare and precious, blooming rose,
Each letter a petal, delicate and fair,
A name so beautiful, beyond compare.

In the tapestry of names, Elizabeth stands tall,
A beacon of beauty, a name for all,

With a legacy that spans the earth and sky,
Elizabeth, a name that will never die.
 So let us raise our voices and sing,
Of Elizabeth, a name fit for a queen,
With every syllable, a story to be told,
Elizabeth, a name worth more than gold.

SIXTEEN

PRECIOUS THAN GOLD

Elizabeth, a name that dances on the tongue,
A symphony of sounds, a melody unsung,
In every letter, a tale of strength and might,
A name that shines like stars in the darkest night.

From the hills of Scotland to the shores of Spain,
Elizabeth, a name that will forever reign,
With a grace that captivates every heart,
A name that's been cherished from the very start.

In the tapestry of time, Elizabeth's name weaves,
A legacy of love, hope, and dreams,
Each letter a brushstroke in a masterpiece divine,
A name that sparkles like a rare and precious wine.

In the whispers of the wind, Elizabeth's name is heard,
A symphony of secrets, a song without a word,

With a power that echoes through the ages,
A name that's etched on history's sacred pages.
　So let us raise our voices and proclaim,
Elizabeth, a name that kindles every flame,
With every syllable, a promise to behold,
Elizabeth, a name more precious than gold.

SEVENTEEN

OH, ELIZABETH

Oh, Elizabeth, a name so fair and bright,
In every syllable, a world of grace and light.
With each letter, a story untold,
A legacy of strength and beauty to behold.

Elegant and regal, like a queen of old,
In every heart, your name takes hold.
A melody of joy, a symphony of love,
A name that soars high on the wings of a dove.

In gardens of words, your name blooms,
A tapestry of colors, a thousand perfumes.
A name that whispers through the ancient trees,
And dances in the breeze, with effortless ease.

Elizabeth, a treasure trove of dreams,
A river flowing with endless streams.
In every verse, your name finds its place,
A muse for poets, a beacon of grace.

So let us raise our voices high,
And sing the praises of Elizabeth, nigh.
For in this name, a universe unfurls,
A name that shines, and forever swirls.

Oh, Elizabeth, in your name we find,
A world of wonder, pure and kind.
A name that echoes through the ages past,
And in our hearts, will forever last.

EIGHTEEN

BOUNDLESS SERENITY

Elizabeth, a name like a symphony of stars,
A tapestry of dreams woven with cosmic bars.
In each syllable, a universe is spun,
A name that dances with the moon and the sun.

In the garden of names, yours stands tall,
A melody of elegance, enchanting all.
With each breath, a new story unfolds,
A name that sparkles, a name that beholds.

Elizabeth, a word that tastes like honey,
A name that paints the sky with colors so sunny.
In every letter, a legend takes flight,
A name that conquers the darkest night.

Like a phoenix rising from the ashes of time,
In your name, a legacy so sublime.
A name that whispers secrets of old,
A name that shines brighter than gold.

In the tapestry of existence, your name weaves,
A symphony of hope, a promise that cleaves.
Elizabeth, a name that echoes through eternity,
A name that holds the key to boundless serenity.
So let us raise our voices and sing,
Of Elizabeth, a name that forever will ring.
In every heartbeat, in every breath,
Your name, Elizabeth, conquers death.

NINETEEN

CELEBRATE YOU

Elizabeth, a name so grand
In every way, she takes a stand
A symphony of syllables, a melody of letters
In every verse, her name is better
In gardens, she's a blooming rose
In mountains, she's a peak that grows
Her name echoes in the halls of time
In every rhythm, it's so sublime
Elizabeth, a name of grace
In every step, she leaves a trace
A tapestry of triumph and might
In every dawn and every night
From ancient lands to modern days
Her name resounds in countless ways
In every tale, she takes her place
A name of beauty, a name of grace

So here's to Elizabeth, so fair
In every heart, she's always there
A name that shines, a name that's true
In every word, we celebrate you

TWENTY

REIGNS SUPREME

Elizabeth, a name of regal charm
In every verse, it causes a warm
And radiant glow, like the sun's embrace
A name that holds both power and grace
In fields of gold, she's a shimmering light
In oceans deep, she's a beacon so bright
Her name dances on the winds of fate
In every story, it's never late
Elizabeth, a name that weaves
A tapestry of dreams and believes
In every heart, it finds a home
A name that's meant to freely roam
From castles old to cities new
Her name stands strong, forever true
In every echo, it rings with pride
A name that no one can divide

So here's to Elizabeth, so dear
In every smile, she's always near
A name that sparkles, a name that gleams
In every world, it reigns supreme

TWENTY-ONE

HERE'S TO THE ELIZABETHS

In the realm of names, there's one that reigns supreme,
A regal moniker, fit for a queen, or so it may seem.
Elizabeth, a name that carries history's weight,
A tapestry of tales, both humble and great.

From the Hebrew, it comes, meaning "God's promise" so divine,
A name that echoes through the corridors of time.
It speaks of strength and grace, a timeless elegance,
A name that holds within it, a quiet resilience.

In the annals of lore, there's many an Elizabeth to find,
Each one a portrait of a unique, brilliant mind.
From poets to queens, and scholars to saints,

The name Elizabeth weaves through countless restraints.

It speaks of nobility, of wisdom, and might,
A name that shines in both darkness and light.
It carries a legacy, a story to tell,
Of women who conquered, against the odds, they befell.

So here's to the Elizabeths, past, present, and yet to come,
May your name be a banner, in battles, yet won.
For in each syllable, there's a universe to explore,
A name that's worth cherishing, now and forevermore.

TWENTY-TWO

ROSES IN BLOOM

Elizabeth, a name that dances on the tongue,
A melody of syllables, a symphony unsung.
It whispers of regal gardens and ancient lore,
A name that opens portals to worlds unknown.

In the tapestry of time, it stands as a beacon,
A name that resonates, in each verse we reckon.
From the courts of old to modern-day dreams,
Elizabeth, a name that echoes through streams.

It carries the fragrance of roses in bloom,
A name that adorns every corner of the room.
With each letter, a story unfolds,
Of courage, of grace, of tales untold.

Elizabeth, a name that wears many crowns,
In its embrace, both thorns and renown.
It speaks of resilience, of strength untold,
A name that weaves through history, bold and old.

So here's to the Elizabeths, past and present,
Whose name is a testament, ever effervescent.
May it echo through the corridors of time,
A name that in every heart, will forever chime.

TWENTY-THREE

ONE OF A KIND

Elizabeth, oh noble and fair,
Thy name doth fill the very air,
With regal grace and timeless charm,
A name that we cannot help but disarm.

In realms of old and tales untold,
Thy name doth shine like precious gold,
A beacon of hope, a symbol of might,
Guiding us through the darkest night.

Elizabeth, a name of strength and grace,
In every heart, it finds a place,
A melody that soothes the soul,
A name that makes us feel whole.

From Elizabethan times to modern days,
Thy name resounds in countless ways,
A name of queens and leaders bold,
A name that history doth enfold.

Oh Elizabeth, in thee we find,
A name that's rare and one of a kind,
So let us raise our voices high,
And celebrate thee, till the end of time.

For in the name Elizabeth, we see,
A world of possibility,
A name that's filled with love and light,
A name that shines so pure and bright.

TWENTY-FOUR

RESONATES

In the realm of appellations, Elizabeth doth dance,
A moniker that weaves a tale, a name of sweet romance.
Beneath the moonlit whispers, its meaning takes its flight,
A symphony of syllables, a serenade in the night.

Elizabeth, a vessel of regality and grace,
Her essence, a tapestry woven in celestial space.
A melange of echoes from eras long past,
In her name, the echoes of history cast.

A herald of triumph, a bearer of truth,
Elizabeth, the embodiment of eternal youth.
In her, echoes of queens who once held sway,
Their echoes linger in the fabric of the day.

A cascade of letters, a river of sound,
Elizabeth, in her, universes are found.

Her name, an anthem sung by the cosmic choir,
A tapestry of dreams, a flame to inspire.
    Through the corridors of time, Elizabeth strides,
A timeless name where destiny abides.
In every syllable, a universe unfolds,
A name that echoes, a story that molds.
    Elizabeth, a symphony in the language of the soul,
A name that resonates, making the universe whole.

TWENTY-FIVE

GLOWS

Oh, Elizabeth, your name inspires delight,
A symphony of syllables, a melody so bright.
In every consonant and every vowel,
Lies a story, a legend, a timeless cowl.

Elegant and regal, like a queen in her domain,
Your name exudes grace, in sunshine and in rain.
It dances off the tongue with a lyrical flow,
A name so enchanting, it steals the show.

From the pages of history to the present day,
Elizabeth, your name stands tall in every way.
It echoes through the corridors of time,
A name so divine, so sublime.

In gardens of words, your name blooms with grace,
A flower of language, in every place.
It whispers of strength and whispers of love,
A name so celestial, it shines above.

Oh, Elizabeth, in every letter and line,
Your name is a treasure, a rare find.
So here's to you, Elizabeth, in poetry and prose,
A name that sparkles, a name that glows.

TWENTY-SIX

MELODIC CHIME

In realms where echoes whisper names divine,
Elizabeth emerges, a poetic design.
A symphony of syllables in graceful ballet,
A sonnet woven in twilight's gentle sway.

Beneath celestial tapestries, her essence blooms,
A cosmic dance, where starlight consumes.
Her name, a sonorous river, winding through time,
A kaleidoscope of echoes, a melodic chime.

In gardens of language, petals unfold,
Each syllable a tale, a narrative bold.
Elizabeth, the muse of yore,
A narrative spun, an ancient lore.

Through moonlit verses, she pirouettes,
A linguistic ballet that none forgets.
Her essence, a quill in the poet's hand,
Painting verses on the canvas of the grand.

Not merely letters, but whispers of soul,
In the lexicon of being, a narrative whole.
A phoenix rising, in linguistic flight,
Elizabeth, a constellation of night.

In the tapestry of language, she weaves her rhyme,
A cadence of epochs, transcending time.
Oh, Elizabeth, a poetic constellation,
In the vast cosmos of linguistic creation.

TWENTY-SEVEN

EPOCHS AND EPOCHS

In the cosmic dance of appellations, behold,
Elizabeth, a sonorous saga beautifully told.
A melodic dance, syllables twirl and sway,
Her name, an ode to dawn's first light array.

In the tapestry of etymology, a tale unfurls,
Each letter a luminescent gem that swirls.
A symphony of consonants, a lyrical grace,
Elizabeth, a poetic embrace.

Amid the celestial ballet, where meanings bloom,
Her name resonates like a fragrant perfume.
A whispered sonnet in the zephyr's embrace,
A harmonious echo, traversing time and space.

Through epochs and epochs, she strides,
A linguistic comet in celestial tides.
Elizabeth, the enchantress of uttered dreams,
A constellation in the vast linguistic streams.

    Her syllables, like stardust, paint the night,
A cosmic sonnet, an ethereal light.
In the lexicon of existence, she finds her place,
Elizabeth, the embodiment of linguistic grace.

    As ink dances upon the parchment's scroll,
Her name, a lyrical anthem, takes its toll.
A symphony of letters, a poetic trance,
Elizabeth, the eternal linguistic dance.

TWENTY-EIGHT

TRANSCENDING YEARS

In realms where shadows gently waltz,
A name emerges, a tale exalts.
Elizabeth, a melody on the lips,
A symphony of echoes, fate equips.

Beneath the boughs, where dreams entwine,
She is the whisper, the elusive sign.
In twilight's dance, a clandestine spell,
Elizabeth, the enigma, where legends swell.

A phoenix rising from embers unseen,
Her essence, a kaleidoscope serene.
Mystique cloaked in silken veils,
A mosaic of stories, where time prevails.

Through labyrinthine corridors of yore,
She strides, a sovereign forevermore.

A rhapsody written in celestial ink,
Elizabeth, the celestial link.

In gardens of prose, where verses bloom,
She is the quasar, dispelling gloom.
A voyage through cosmic constellations,
Her aura, a tapestry of endless variations.

Behold the tapestry woven with grace,
Elizabeth, the sovereign in time's embrace.
A sonnet sung by celestial spheres,
Her name, an anthem, transcending years.

TWENTY-NINE

ODYSSEY IN ETERNITY

In the cosmic ballet, a whispered refrain,
Elizabeth, a sonnet in nature's grand terrain.
A symphony of echoes, as stars conspire,
Her name, an ethereal flame, a celestial lyre.

Beneath the moon's clandestine glow,
A serenade of secrets, she does bestow.
A riddle wrapped in twilight's gown,
Elizabeth, the muse of the cosmic town.

Through veils of time, a dance unfolds,
Her essence, a saga, forever told.
A nebula's grace in every syllable,
She's the mystic journey, ineffable.

In the garden of existence, she blooms,
Elizabeth, the harbinger of poetic dooms.
A phoenix reborn in each dawn's glow,
Her presence, a kaleidoscope's gentle flow.

Across the astral expanse, she strides,
A constellation's secret, where destiny hides.
A tapestry woven with stardust and dreams,
Elizabeth, the luminary, as celestial beams.

Behold the echo of her name in the cosmic hum,
A celestial dance where mysteries become.
Elizabeth, the cosmic serendipity,
Her name, an odyssey in eternity.

THIRTY

HER NAME

In the tapestry of existence, a melody unfolds,
Elizabeth, a reverie, a tale yet to be told.
Beneath the moon's soft luminescent art,
She's the clandestine rhythm, the soul's counterpart.

Through the corridors of time, she weaves,
A cosmic sonnet, where every heartbeat cleaves.
A whisper in the zephyr, a secret in the breeze,
Elizabeth, the harbinger of tranquil seas.

In the garden of names, a bloom rare,
Her essence, a celestial flare.
A dance with shadows, a waltz with light,
She's the echo of dreams in the tranquil night.

Within the celestial theatre, she takes her bow,
A stellar performance, a serenade somehow.
A phoenix in the symphony of dawn,
Elizabeth, the ethereal queen, silently drawn.

Her name, a symphony of constellations bright,
A voyage through galaxies, a celestial flight.
In the lexicon of stars, where meanings blend,
Elizabeth, the cosmic poem, with no end.

THIRTY-ONE

SOVEREIGN

In the cosmic tale, where galaxies sway,
Elizabeth emerges, a celestial ballet.
A melody woven through the fabric of night,
Her name, an aurora, shimmering with light.

In the garden of echoes, where whispers bloom,
She's the clandestine fragrance, dispelling gloom.
A serenade of stardust in the twilight air,
Elizabeth, the ethereal, beyond compare.

Through time's labyrinth, a dance unfolds,
Her essence, a symphony of stories retold.
A mosaic of dreams painted on the cosmic breeze,
She's the elusive muse, swaying with ease.

In the celestial waltz, where destinies entwine,
Elizabeth, a comet's trail, divine.
A tapestry woven with threads of cosmic grace,
Her name, an anthem echoing through space.

Beneath the moon's soft glow, she enchants,
A celestial sonnet, where eternity chants.
A phoenix rising from the embers of the unknown,
Elizabeth, the cosmic sovereign on her throne.

Behold the celestial canvas, where her name's inscribed,
A timeless saga in which dreams are scribed.
Elizabeth, the cosmic poem unfurled,
Her name, a celestial whisper in the cosmic world.

THIRTY-TWO

LEGACY

In realms where echoes of antiquity dance,
A name unfolds, a mystic trance.
Elizabeth, a tapestry of regal grace,
Inscribed in history's noble embrace.

In gardens of language, petals unfurl,
Each syllable, a gem, a luminescent swirl.
Whispers of antiquity, a symphony grand,
Echo through time, across the land.

A moniker adorned with majesty's gown,
Inscribing narratives of renown.
A serenade of letters, an eloquent spell,
In the lexicon's ballad, it doth dwell.

Elizabeth, a voyage through linguistic seas,
Each phoneme, a vessel, tales to appease.
From ancient scrolls to modern lore,
A name's cadence, an everlasting core.

In realms of etymology's poetic verse,
Elizabeth, a sonnet, a universe.
A kaleidoscope of meanings untold,
A timeless saga, an enigma to behold.
　　Thus, in the tapestry of linguistic art,
Elizabeth, a masterpiece, a work of heart.
A symphony of vowels, a consonantal embrace,
A name, a legacy, in the grandeur of space.

THIRTY-THREE

CHEERS

In the cosmic ballet, Elizabeth pirouettes,
A sonnet whispered in linguistic vignettes.
Her syllabic rhythm, a celestial dance,
A tapestry woven with letters, a chance.
   Through the epochs, she echoes in the breeze,
A name that sails across linguistic seas.
Meaning unfurls like petals in spring,
A melodic symphony, an eternal fling.
   In the mosaic of language, she takes her stand,
A mystic anthem, notes written in the sand.
Each consonant, a herald, each vowel a plea,
Elizabeth, a whisper in eternity.
   From ancient scrolls to the modern scroll,
Her resonance weaves, an enchanting stroll.
In the pages of time, her chapters unfold,
A saga of meanings, a story retold.

Elizabeth, an oracle in the script of fate,
Her essence, a melody, a name so great.
In the verse of existence, she's a sweet refrain,
A linguistic legacy, an immortal gain.

Her meaning, a journey through realms untold,
A harmonious echo, a story to be extolled.
Elizabeth, a name that time endears,
In the symphony of life, she reverberates cheers.

THIRTY-FOUR

TALE TO BE TOLD

In realms of eloquence, where verses dance,
Elizabeth, a name, in brilliance, doth enhance.
A symphony of syllables, a linguistic trance,
In the poetic tapestry, she takes her stance.

With letters like pearls, strung in a name,
Elizabeth, the muse, in language aflame.
Her essence, a sonnet, in an artful claim,
A lexical waltz, a lyrical acclaim.

In gardens of lexicon, where words unfold,
Elizabeth, a bloom, in narratives untold.
Her consonants and vowels, a tale to be told,
In the cosmic library, her story, bold.

Through the quill's ballet, she pirouettes,
Elizabeth, the sonneteer, in poetic vignettes.
Each syllable, a serenade the heart begets,
In the parchment of language, her spirit resets.

Oh, Elizabeth, in linguistic realms, thee reign,
A sovereign of syntax, in an eternal domain.
In the cathedral of words, thou dost sustain,
A symphonic sonnet, an everlasting refrain.

THIRTY-FIVE

LOVE AND POWER

Elizabeth, oh name so divine
In each letter, a tale does entwine
E - for the enchantment you exude
L - for the luminescence in your attitude
I - for the intelligence you wield with grace
Z - for the zest that lights up your face
A - for the allure that draws all near
B - for the brilliance that banishes fear
E - for the empathy in your kind heart
T - for the tenacity that sets you apart
H - for the heroism in all that you do
In each way, Elizabeth, we honor you
In history's annals, your name prevails
In every story, your spirit hails
From ancient courts to modern day
Your name resounds in every way

    Elizabeth, in each syllable, a melody
Of resilience, beauty, and bravery
In each whisper, a promise of might
A name that shines through day and night
    Let us raise our voices with pride
In celebration of Elizabeth, far and wide
For in this name, a legacy is unfurled
Of love and power that spans the world

ABOUT THE CREATOR

Walter the Educator is one of the pseudonyms for Walter Anderson. Formally educated in Chemistry, Business, and Education, he is an educator, an author, a diverse entrepreneur, and he is the son of a disabled war veteran. "Walter the Educator" shares his time between educating and creating. He holds interests and owns several creative projects that entertain, enlighten, enhance, and educate, hoping to inspire and motivate you.

Follow, find new works, and stay up to date
with Walter the Educator™
at WaltertheEducator.com

www.ingramcontent.com/pod-product-compliance
Lightning Source LLC
LaVergne TN
LVHW052000060526
838201LV00059B/3755